The Latent Power
of
The Soul

The Latent Power of The Soul

WATCHMAN NEE

Translated from the Chinese

Christian Fellowship Publishers, Inc.
New York

Available from the Publishers at:

11515 Allecingie Parkway
Richmond, Virginia 23235

PRINTED IN U.S.A.

CONTENTS

Scripture quotations are from the
American Standard Version (1901)
of the Bible
unless otherwise indicated.

Preface

When in 1924 I first called the attention of God's children to the dividing of spirit and soul, many well-disposed brethren thought of it as merely a dispute over words having no great significance. What they failed to see was that our conflict is not concerned with word but with that which lies behind. The spirit and the soul are two totally different organs: one belongs to God, while the other belongs to man. By whatever names one may call them, they are completely distinct in substance. The peril of the believer is to confuse the spirit for the soul and the soul for the spirit, and so be deceived into accepting the counterfeit of evil spirits to the unsettling of God's work.

This series of articles had originally been intended to be written immediately following the completion (in 1928) of *The Spiritual Man*. But because of physical weakness and the heavy burden of other service, I was only able to have them published in last year's issues of *Revival* magazine. In response to the request of its readers, I now put forth this booklet.

The greatest advantage in knowing the difference between spirit and soul is in perceiving the latent power of the soul and in understanding its falsification of the power of the Holy Spirit. Such knowledge is not theoretical but practical in helping people to walk in God's way.

Just last night I was reading what F. B. Meyer once said in a meeting shortly before his earthly departure. Here is a section of it: "This is an amazing fact that never has there been so much spiritualism outside the church of Christ as is found today . . . Is it not factual that in the lower part of our human nature the stimulation of the soul is quite prevailing? Nowadays the atmosphere is so charged with the commotion of all kinds of counterfeit that the Lord seems to be calling the church to come to a higher ground."* Today's situation is perilous. May we "prove all things; hold fast that which is good" (1 Thess. 5.21). Amen.

Watchman Nee
March 8, 1933

---

*Since the original quotation could not be found, this portion has been freely translated from the Chinese.—*Translator*

The Latent Power of the Soul

And the merchants of the earth weep and mourn over her, for no man buyeth their merchandise any more; merchandise of gold, and silver, and precious stone, and pearls . . . and cattle, and sheep, and merchandise of horses and chariots and slaves (Gr. *bodies*); and souls of men. (Rev. 18.11-13) Please note here that in this passage the list of merchandise commences with gold and silver and ends with souls of men. Gold and silver, horses and chariots are all natural commodities which can be bartered. Even slaves can be bartered or traded—yet this is a trading in human *bodies*. Further, though, is an exchanging of the *souls* of men as merchandise.

So also it is written, The first man Adam became a living soul. The last Adam became a life-giving spirit. Howbeit that is not first which is spiritual, but that which is natural; then that which is spiritual. (1 Cor. 15.45,46)

> And Jehovah God formed man of the dust of the
> ground, and breathed into his nostrils the breath of
> life; and man became a living soul. (Gen. 2.7)

Over the past two years I have felt strongly the
need of giving such a message as will now be given. It
is a message both intricate and profound. It will not
be easy for the speaker to speak nor for the hearers to
understand. For this reason, I did not insert this message into Part Three of *The Spiritual Man*.* Yet I
have always felt I should give it, especially after
having read various books and magazines and having
had contact to a certain extent with the people of
this world. I sense how precious is the truth we are
privileged to know. In view of the current situation
and tendency of the church as well as of the world,
we are constrained to share what is given to us. Otherwise we will be hiding the lamp under a bushel.

What I would mention in the message for our
consideration today concerns spiritual warfare and its
relation to the end of this age. Now for the sake of
those who have not read *The Spiritual Man*, I will
briefly touch on the trilogy of spirit, soul, and body.

Trilogy of Spirit, Soul, and Body

"And Jehovah God formed man of the dust of

---

*Watchman Nee, *The Spiritual Man*. 3 vols. New York, Christian
Fellowship Publishers, 1968. Translated from the Chinese.

the ground" (Gen. 2.7). This refers to the human body. "And breathed into his nostrils the breath of life." This describes how God gave spirit to man; it was Adam's spirit. So man's body was formed of the dust of the ground, and man's spirit was given to him by God. "And man became a living soul." After the breath of life had entered into his nostrils man became a living soul. The spirit, the soul, and the body are three separate entities. "May your spirit and soul and body be preserved entire" (1 Thess. 5.23). The spirit is God-given; the soul is a living soul; and the body is God-formed.

According to common understanding the soul is our personality. When the spirit and the body were joined, man became a living soul. The characteristic of the angels is spirit and that of the lower animals such as beasts is flesh. We humans have both spirit and body; but our characteristic is neither spirit nor body but soul. We have a living soul. Hence the Bible calls man soul. For example, when Jacob went down into Egypt with his family, the Scriptures tell us that "all the souls of the house of Jacob, that came into Egypt, were threescore and ten" (Gen. 46.27). Again, those who had received Peter's word on Pentecost were baptised and "there were added unto them in that day about three thousand souls" (Acts 2.41). Hence soul stands for our personality, for what makes us as man.

What are the various functions of spirit, soul, and body? These have already been explained in Part One of *The Spiritual Man.* But I was most happy one day to find on the bookshelf a volume of Andrew Murray's writings in which is to be found an explanation of the spirit, soul, and body in the appended notes that is quite similar to our interpretation. What follows is a quotation from one of the notes:

In the history of man's creation we read, 'The Lord God formed man of the dust of the ground'—thus was his *body* made—'and breathed into his nostrils the breath' or spirit 'of life': thus his *spirit* came from God; 'and man became a *living soul*.' The spirit quickening the body made man a living soul, a living person with the consciousness of himself. The soul was the meeting-place, the point of union between body and spirit. Through the *body*, man, the living soul, stood related to the external world of sense; could influence it, or be influenced by it. Through the *spirit* he stood related to the spiritual world and the Spirit of God, whence he had his origin; could be the recipient and the minister of its life and power. Standing thus midway between two worlds, belonging to both, the *soul* had the power of determining itself, of choosing or refusing the objects by which it was surrounded, and to which it stood related.

In the constitution of these three parts of man's nature, the spirit, as linking him with the Divine, was the highest; the body, connecting him with the sensible and animal, the lowest; intermediate stood the soul, partaker of the nature of the others, the bond that united them and through which they could act on each other. Its work, as the central power, was to maintain them in their due relation; to keep the body, as the lowest, in subjection to the spirit; itself to receive through the spirit, as the higher, from the Divine Spirit what was waiting *(sic)* it for its perfection: and so to pass down, even to the body, that by which it might be partaker of the Spirit's perfection and become a spiritual body.*

What is the spirit? That which makes us conscious of God and relates us to God is the spirit. What is the soul? It is that which relates us to ourselves and gives us self-consciousness. What is the body? It causes us to be related to the world. C. I. Scofield, in his reference Bible, explains that the spirit gives God-consciousness, the soul self-consciousness, the body world-consciousness. Horse and ox are not conscious of God because they have no spirit. They are only conscious of their own beings. The body causes us to sense the world—such as our seeing the things of the world, our feeling hot or cold, and so forth.

What is mentioned above refers to the functions of spirit, soul, and body. I will now come to the very important problem here. Many view this matter of spirit, soul, and body as being related only to spiritual life; but we need to realize that it is also relevant to spiritual work and warfare. We tend to compare ourselves as being almost equal to Adam before his fall.

---

*Andrew Murray, *The Spirit of Christ*. Fort Washington, Pa., Christian Literature Crusade, 1964. Note C: The Place of the Indwelling, p.227-228.

We assume that since we are human beings just as Adam was, there is not too much difference between us. We think that what *we* cannot do, neither could Adam do. But we do not see that there are two things here: (a) that on the one hand, it is true that we cannot do what Adam could *not* do; yet also (b) that we cannot do what Adam *could* do. I am afraid we do not realize how capable Adam was. If we study the Bible carefully we will understand what kind of man Adam actually was before his fall.

Adam's Authority and Physical Prowess

"And God created man in his own image, in the image of God created he him; male and female created he them. And God blessed them: and God said unto them, Be fruitful, and multiply, and replenish the earth, and subdue it; and have dominion over the fish of the sea, and over the birds of the heavens, and over every living thing that moveth upon the earth" (Gen. 1.27,28). Have dominion over the earth, says God.

Friends, have you ever thought how immense the earth is? Suppose a master asks a servant to manage two houses. He makes the appointment on the basis of the latter's ability to take care of them. No one servant is able to handle all the houses located on a given lane, for he cannot do what is beyond his ability. A hard master may demand his servant to do a little more than his duty requires, but never will he demand his servant to undertake anything beyond his ability. Would God, then, ask Adam to do what he was incapable of doing? We can therefore conclude that if Adam was capable of managing the earth, his prowess was most certainly superior to ours today. He had power, ability, and skill. He received all of these abilities freshly from the Creator.

Although we may not rate Adam's power as being a *billion* times over ours, we can nonetheless safely reckon it to be a *million* times over ours. Else he would not have been able to perform the duty commanded him of God. As for us today, though, if we were required to merely sweep a lane three times daily, we would not be able afterwards to straighten our back. How then could we possibly rule the earth? Yet Adam not only ruled the earth but he also had dominion over the fish of the sea, the birds of the heavens, and every living thing on the earth. To rule is not just to sit by doing nothing. It requires management and work. From a seeing of this we should recognize the superior power which Adam in fact possessed. It far exceeds our present situation.

But do you think that this insight is something new? Actually this is the teaching of the Bible. Before his fall Adam had such strength that he never felt tired after work. It was only after his fall that God told him, "In the sweat of thy face shalt thou eat bread."

Adam's Brain Power and Memory

"And out of the ground Jehovah God formed

every beast of the field, and every bird of the heavens; and brought them unto the man to see what he would call them; and whatsoever the man called every living creature, that was the name thereof" (Gen. 2.19). My friends, is this not marvelous? Suppose you were to take a dictionary and to read all the names of the animals; would you not confess that you could neither recognize nor memorize them all? Yet Adam gave names to all the birds and animals. How intelligent he must have been! Those of us who are not so brilliant would no doubt soon give up the study of zoology once we saw our inability to memorize all the details. But Adam was not one who *memorized* these zoological names; he was the denominator, for he *gave* names to all. Hereby do we know how rich and perfect was Adam's rational power.

Adam's Managerial Power

"And Jehovah God took the man and put him into the garden of Eden to dress it and to keep it" (Gen. 2.15). From looking into how Adam governed the earth let us now dwell somewhat on the things which God charged him to do. God commanded him to dress the garden of Eden. This needed to be done systematically. How big was the garden? Genesis 2.10-14 mentions four rivers; namely, Pishon, Gihon, Hiddekel and Euphrates. They all flowed from Eden and divided into four river regions. Can you imagine now how big the garden was? How strong must Adam be to be charged with dressing a land which was surrounded by four rivers! He was not only to dress it but also to keep it; to keep the garden from being invaded by the enemy. Therefore the power which Adam had in that day must have been tremendous. He must have been a man with astounding ability. All his powers were inherent in his living soul. We may look upon Adam's power as supernatural and miraculous, but so far as Adam was concerned these abilities were not miraculous but human, not supernatural but natural.

Did Adam use up all his powers on that day? From what can be seen in our study of Genesis, he had not exhausted his power. For after he was newly created by God, but before he could manifest all his abilities, he fell.

What was the bait which the enemy used in enticing Eve? What did the enemy promise her? It was this: "In the day ye eat thereof, then your eyes shall be opened, and ye shall be as God, knowing good and evil" (Gen. 3.5). "Be as God" was the enemy's promise. He told Eve that not withstanding the power which she already possessed there was still a great chasm between her and God, but that if she ate this fruit she would then have God's authority, wisdom, and power. And on that day Eve was tempted and fell.

The Power God Gave to Adam

We are not, by our probing in this fashion, being

inordinately curious; we only desire to know what God actually gave to Adam. "And God said, Let us make man in our image, after our likeness" (Gen. 1.26). The words "image" and "likeness" may seem to be alike in meaning and may therefore appear repetitious. But in Hebrew the word "image" does not point to physical likeness, rather it denotes moral or spiritual similarity. Someone has put it as: "change into likeness"; that is, "to be conformed to a likeness". The purpose in God creating man is for man to be transformed according to His image. God wanted Adam to be like Him. The devil said, "Ye shall be as God." But God's original intention was that Adam should be transformed to become like Him.

From this we conclude that before the fall Adam had in him the power to become like God. He possessed a hidden ability which made it possible for him to become like God. He was already like Him in outward appearance, but he was ordained by God to become like Him morally (I use the word "morally" to indicate that which is above the material, not what merely points to man's good behavior). Thus are we shown how much loss mankind has suffered through the fall. The magnitude of the damage is probably beyond our imagination.

The Fall of Man

Adam is a soul. His spirit and body are joined in his soul. That astonishing power which we have just mentioned is present in Adam's soul. In other words, the living soul, which is the result of the coming together of the spirit and the body, possesses unthinkable supernatural power. At the fall, though, the power which distinquishes Adam from us is lost. Yet this does not mean there is no longer such power; it only denotes that though this ability is still in man, it is nonetheless "frozen" or immobilized. According to Genesis 6, after the fall man becomes flesh. The flesh envelops the whole being and subjugates him. Man was originally a living soul; now, having fallen, he becomes flesh. His soul had been meant to submit to the spirit's control; now it is subject to the dominion of the flesh. Hence the Lord said, "My Spirit shall not strive with man for ever, for that he also is flesh" (Gen. 6.3). When God here mentioned man, He called him flesh, for in His eyes that was now what he was. Consequently it is recorded in the Bible that "all flesh had corrupted their way upon the earth" (Gen. 6.12); and again, "upon the flesh of man shall it (the holy anointing oil, representing in type the Holy Spirit) not be poured" (Ex. 30.32); and further, "by the works of the law shall no flesh be justified in His sight" (Rom. 3.20).

Why do I dwell at some length on this? In Revelation 18 things are mentioned which shall come to pass in the last days. I indicated at the very beginning how man's soul will become a commodity in Babylon—that which can be sold and bought. But why is man's soul treated as a commodity? Because Satan and his puppet the Antichrist wish to use the human soul as an instrument for their activities at the end of this age. When Adam fell in the garden of Eden his power was immobilized. He had not lost this power altogether, only it was now buried within him. He had become flesh, and his flesh now enclosed tightly this marvelous power within it. Generation has succeeded generation with the result that this primordial ability of Adam has become a "latent" force in his descendants. It has turned to become a kind of "hidden" power. It is not lost to man, it is simply bound up by the flesh.

Today in each and every person who lives on earth lies this Adamic power, though it is confined in him and is not able to freely express itself. Yet such power is in every man's soul just as it was in Adam's soul at the beginning. Since today's soul is under siege by the flesh, this power is likewise confined by the flesh. The work of the devil nowadays is to stir up man's soul and to release this latent power within it as a deception for spiritual power. The reason for my mentioning these things is to warn ourselves of the special relationship between man's soul and Satan in the last days.

We have already seen how Adam possessed special supernatural ability, though in actuality what he had was not at all special or supernatural, however much it may appear that way to us today. Before his fall Adam could quite naturally exercise this ability with ease, since it was embodied in his soul. But after his fall, this power of his was interned by his body. Formerly the body was a help to Adam's powerful soul;

now the soul had fallen, and his power was circumscribed by the shell of the flesh. Satan, however, attempts to break open this fleshly shell and to release the power dormant in man's soul in order to gain control over man. Many do not understand this strategy, being deceived into accepting it as of God.

Viewing Religiously

Yet this does not happen in Christianity alone. The Babylonians, the Arabs, the Buddhists, the Taoists, and the Hindus all try in their respective way to release the power which Adam has left to our soul. In any religion, using whatever means or ways of instruction, there stands a common principle behind all their apparent differences. This common principle is to aim at overcoming the outward flesh so as to deliver the soul power from all kinds of bondage for freer expression. Some lessons of instruction given in these religions are directed at destroying the obstruction of the body, some at uniting the body and the soul, while some are aimed at strengthening the soul through training and thus enabling it to overcome the body. Whatever the ways may be, the principle behind them all is the same. It is important to know this or else we will be deceived.

I do not know how people are informed of the marvelous energy dormant in man's soul, the release of which, presently bound by the flesh, will result in the display of miraculous power even to the attaining of the status of a "fairy" or "buddha". Probably they are all informed by the devil, the evil spirit. Their elucidations may vary, nevertheless the underlying principle is the same, which is, the use of special means to release the power of the soul. They may not employ, as used by us, this terminology of soul power; yet the fact is unmistakable. For example, in Buddhism and Taoism, and even in some sects of Christianity, special supernatural power is available to all of them to perform miracles in the healing of diseases and in predicting the future.

Take as an instance the ascetic practices and breathings of Taoism or even the simplest form of abstract meditation: these are all done according to the one principle of subjugating the body under the soul with the purpose of releasing the latter's power. No wonder many miraculous things do happen which we cannot simply dismiss as superstition. Buddhism was originally atheistic. Gautama Siddharta was an atheist. This is the consensus of many scholars and critics on the teaching of Buddhism. He believed in the soul's transmigration as well as in nirvana*. Now I have no intention here of lecturing on Buddhism; I only wish to explain why and how many a wonder has been performed in this religion.

In Buddhism there is the teaching on escaping the

---

*That state, according to *The American Heritage Dictionary of the English Language*, "of absolute blessedness, characterized by release from the cycle of reincarnations and attained through the extinction of self."—*Translator*

world. Those who take the Buddhist vow must abstain from marriage and meat. They must not kill any living thing. Through ascetic practices they may eventually attain to the elimination of all food. Some monks of high degree can even pierce the unknown past and predict the future. They perform many wonders by Buddhist magic. When what they call their "heart blood" flushes, they are able to foretell the things to come. The engaging in all these different kinds of abstinences and ascetic practices flows from one single governing principle: the Buddhist is attempting to break all physical and material bonds so as to get his soul power released.

I know some people, my seniors in age, who joined the Unity Club. They and their fellow-Club members practice abstract meditation and so forth. They tell me that each degree they enter into has its own magnitude of light. The light they perceive follows the truth they penetrate. I believe in what they say, for they are able to be liberated from the suppression of the body and so release the power which Adam possessed before his fall. There is really nothing extraordinary about it.

The modern-day Church of Christ, Scientist was founded by Mrs. Mary Baker Eddy. She denied the existence of sickness, pain, sin, and death (though Mrs. Eddy has already died). Since according to her teaching there is no such thing as sickness, whenever one is sick he only needs to exercise his mind against any recognition of pain and he will be healed. This means, then, that if one believes in no sickness he will not be sick. So too, if he does not believe in sin he will not sin. By training man's will, mind, and emotion to the point of absolutely denying the existence of these things—viewing them as false and deceptive— he will find them nonexistent indeed.

When this teaching was first promulgated, it was opposed by many people. Physicians especially opposed it, for if this were true, then there would be no need for physicians. Yet following their examination of those people healed by the Christian Scientist, these doctors were unable to repudiate it as false. Consequently, more and more people believe; even many famous scientists and physicians embrace this teaching. This is not at all surprising, though, since there is a reservoir of tremendous power in the soul just waiting to be released from the confines of the flesh.

Viewing Scientifically

Let us now view this matter scientifically. The field of psychology has undertaken unprecedented research in the modern age. What is psychology? The word itself is the combination of two Greek words: "psyche" which means soul and "logia" which means discourse. Hence psychology is "the science of the soul". The research engaged in by modern scientists is but a probing into the soul part of our being. It is limited to that part, the spirit not being touched.

Modern parapsychology began with Franz Anton

Mesmer. His first discovery, made in 1778, is now known as mesmerism (hypnotism as practised by Mesmer himself). His disciples excelled him through their own discoveries, just as the green which is derived from the blue excels the blue. Some of their experiments are almost unbelievable in results. Their method not unexpectedly is to discharge that hidden power within man's soul. For example, in clairvoyance (the power to perceive things which are out of the natural range of human senses) or telepathy (communication by scientifically unknown or inexplicable means, as by the exercise of mystic power), people are able to see or hear or smell things thousands of miles away.

It has been said that mesmerism "is the rock from which all mental sciences . . . were hewn."* Before the time of Mesmer psychic research was not an independent branch of science; it occupied only an insignificant place in natural science. But due to these astonishing discoveries, it has become a system of its own.

I wish to draw your attention not to the study of psychology but to the fact that all these miraculous phenomena are obtained through the release of the latent power of man's soul, that ability which was hidden in man after the fall. Why is this called

---

*Mrs. Jessie Penn-Lewis, *Soul and Spirit.* Poole, Dorset, England, Overcomer Literature Trust, 1968?, p.67. Also available in the United States from Christian Literature Crusade, Fort Washington, Pa.

"latent" power? Because in Adam's fall God had not withdrawn from him that "supernatural" power which he once possessed. Instead, this power fell with him and became imprisoned in his body. The power was there; only it could not be expressed. Hence the term latent power.

The phenomena of our human life such as speaking and thinking are abilities which are quite remarkable; but the latent power that is hidden in man is also striking. And were this power to be activated, many more remarkable phenomena would be displayed in our life. The many miraculous occurrences which modern parapsychologists discover in no way attest to their supernatural character. They merely prove that the latent power of the soul may be released by the appropriate means.

> A list of some of the 'discoveries' which followed the obtaining by Mesmer of the basic knowledge of the mysterious forces latent in the human frame, shows how amazingly the movement advanced, once man had obtained the key. In 1784, a pupil of Mesmer's discovered 'clairvoyance' as the result of Mesmeric sleep, and incidentally stumbled upon 'Thought Reading'.*

Telepathy—being communication between mind and mind otherwise than through the known channels of the senses—enables a person to use his own psychic

---

*Penn-Lewis, *op. cit.*, p.67.

force to ascertain another's thought without the need of being told. "Hypnotism, Neurology, and Psychometry . . . and numberless other 'discoveries' followed as the years went by."* Now hypnosis is an artificially induced sleep-like condition in which an individual is extremely responsive to suggestions made by the hypnotist. Not only man, even lower animals can also be hypnotised. And psychometry is

> the discovery that the mind can act outside the human body and that the 'psychometric sensitive' can read the past like an open book. Then came a discovery, called *statuvolism*, signifying a peculiar condition produced by the will, in which the subject can 'throw his mind' to any distant place, and see, hear, feel, smell and taste, what is going on there. Then . . . came a discovery . . . called 'Pathetism' . . . By this the mind could withdraw itself from the consciousness of pain, and cure diseases.
>
> At first, scientific men only followed up these 'discoveries' as branches of Natural Science . . . .*

But due to multiplication of these miraculous phenomena, parapsychology soon became a science itself. To the practitioners of this science these many miraculous phenomena are quite natural. To us believers they are even more natural. For we know they are merely the consequences of the releasing of the latent power of the soul.

------

*Penn-Lewis, *op. cit.*, p.67-68.

Psychologists declare that within man is a tremendous array of power: the power of self-control, creative power, reconstructive power, the power of faith, the power of quickening, the power of revivification. These can all be released by men. One psychology book even goes so far as to proclaim that all humans are gods, only that the god is imprisoned within us. By releasing the god within us we all become gods. How alike are these words to those of Satan!

The Common Rule

Whether it is in China or in Western nations, all these practices of breathing, ascetic exercise, hypnosis, prediction, responses, and communications are but the release and manifestation of the power within. I suppose we have all heard something of the miraculous acts of hypnosis. In China are fortune-tellers whose feats of prediction are well-known. Each day they interview only a few customers. They have devoted much time and energy in perfecting their art. And their predictions are amazingly accurate. Buddhists and Taoists have their miraculous performances too. Though evidence of deception is not lacking, apparently supernatural manifestations are undeniable.

The explanation for these phenomena is simple: they either by chance or at the direction of the evil spirit hit upon some way or ways of ascetic practice that enable them to perform extraordinary feats. Common people do not know they have this power in themselves. Others with some scientific knowledge know this power is hidden in them, though they cannot tell how it is so. We who have been taught of God know that this ability is the latent power of man's soul which is now bound in the flesh through Adam's fall. This power had fallen with man, so that according to God's will it should not be used any further. But it is Satan's desire to develop this latent ability so as to make man feel he is as rich as God in accordance with what Satan had promised. Thus will man worship himself, though indirectly it is a worship of Satan.

Hence Satan is behind all these parapsychic researches. He is trying his best to use the latent energy of the soul to accomplish his goal. For this reason, all who develop their soul power cannot avoid being contacted and used by the evil spirit.

G. H. Pember, in his book *Earth's Earliest Ages*, has stated this matter from still another angle:

> It appears that there are two methods by which men can acquire unlawful power and knowledge, and gain admittance to a prohibited intercourse. He who would follow the first . . . must so bring his body under the control of his own soul that he can project his soul . . . . The development of these faculties is, doubtless, possible but to few, and even in their case can only be compassed by a long and severe course of training, the object of which is, to break down the body to a complete subjection, and to produce a perfect apathy in regard to all the pleasures, pains, and emotions, of this life, so that no disturbing elements

> may ruffle the calm of the aspirant's mind and hinder
> his progress . . . The second method is by a passive
> submission to the control of foreign intelligences....*

What we would especially pay attention to here is
the first method, that is, activating the latent power
of one's own soul. His view coincides with ours completely. The ascetic practices of the Buddhists, the
breathing and abstract meditation of the Taoists, the
meditation and thought concentration of the hypnotists, the silent sitting by those in the Unity Club, and
all the varieties of meditations, contemplations, con-
centrated thought to no thought at all, and hundreds
of similar actions which people practice, follow the
same rule—however varied their knowledge and faith
may be. What all do is nothing more than bring man's
external confused thought, wavy emotion, and weak
will to a place of tranquillity, with his flesh completely subdued, hence making possible the release of
the soul's latent power. The reason this is not mani-
fested in every person is because not all can break
through the barriers of the flesh and bring all common psychic expressions to perfect calmness.

Some Facts

Several years ago I made the acquaintance of an

---

*G. H. Pember, *Earth's Earliest Ages*. New York, Fleming H.
Revell Co., n.d., p.251-254.

Indian. He told me of a friend of his in Hinduism who could reveal secrets of people accurately. Once he wished to test the ability of his Hindu friend. So he invited him to his home, and sure enough the Hindu was able to reveal everything that had been put into each drawer of the home. Later my Indian acquaintance asked his friend to go outside and wait while he wrapped a most valuable object in cloth and paper before placing it in a box and depositing it in a locked drawer. His Hindu friend returned inside and was able to reveal what the valuable object was without error. This was unquestionably due to the exercise of soul power that was able to penetrate all physical barriers.

Mrs. Jessie Penn-Lewis, whom we have quoted earlier, once wrote the following:

> I once met a man in North India, who had access to the highest circles of society in Simla, the summer seat of the Government of India, who told me one evening of his connection with the Mahatmas in India and in other countries of Asia. He said that he knew of great political events weeks and months before they came to pass. 'I do not depend for news on telegrams and newspapers. They only record past events, we know events before they take place,' he said. How can a man in London know the events happening in India, and vice-versa? It was explained to me that it was through 'soul-force' being projected by men who knew the secret of the Mahatmas.*

Overcomer magazine for 1921-23, quoted in Mrs. Jessie

In quoting from Wild's *Spiritual Dynamics*, Pember has recorded that an adept

> can consciously see the minds of others. He can act by his soul-force on external spirits. He can accelerate the growth of plants and quench fire; and, like Daniel, subdue ferocious wild beasts. He can send his soul to a distance, and there not only read the thoughts of others, but speak to and touch those distant objects; and not only so, but he can exhibit to his distant friends his spiritual body in the exact likeness of that of the flesh. Moreover . . . the adept . . . can . . . create out of the surrounding multiplex atmosphere the likeness of any physical object, or he can command physical objects to come into his presence.**

The Christian's Attitude

These miraculous phenomena in religion and science are but the manifestation of man's latent power which in turn is used by the evil spirit. They all follow one common rule: to break through the bonds of the flesh and release the power of the soul. The difference between us (the Christians) and them lies in the fact that all our miracles are performed by God

Penn-Lewis, *Soul and Spirit.* Poole, Dorset, England, Overcomer Literature Trust, 1968?, p.55-56. Also available in the United States from Christian Literature Crusade, Fort Washington, Pa.

**Pember, *op. cit.*, p.252.

through the Holy Spirit. Satan makes use of man's soul force to manifest his strength. Man's soul power is Satan's working instrument, through which he works out his evil end.

God, though, never works with man's soul power, for it is unusable to Him. When we are born again, we are born of the Holy Spirit. God works by the Holy Spirit and our renewed spirit. He has no desire to use soul power. Since the fall God has forbidden man to again use his original power of the soul. It is for this reason that the Lord Jesus often declares how we need to lose our soul life, that is, our soul power. God wishes us today not to use this soul power at all.

We cannot say that all the wonders performed in the world are false; we have to acknowledge that many of them are real. But all these phenomena are produced by the latent power of the soul after Adam's fall. As Christians we must be very careful in this last age not to stir up soul's latent energy either purposely or unwittingly.

Let us return again to the Scriptures read at the beginning. We notice that at the end of the age the particular work Satan and the evil spirits under him will do is to trade in man's soul power. The aim is simply to fill this world with the latent power of the soul. One correspondent to the *Overcomer* magazine made the following comparison: "the forces of *psyche* (soul) arrayed against the forces of *pneuma* (spirit)."* All who have spiritual insight and sensi-

---

*As quoted in Penn-Lewis, *op. cit.*, p.55.

tivity know the reality of this statement. Soul power is rushing towards us like a torrent. Making use of science (psychology and parapsychology), religion, and even an ignorant church (in her seeking excessively supernatural manifestations and in her not controlling supernatural gifts according to the guidance of the Bible), Satan is causing this world to be filled with the power of darkness. Yet this is but Satan's last and final preparation for the manifestation of the Antichrist. Those who are truly spiritual (that is, those who reject soul power) sense all around them the acceleration of opposition from the evil spirits. The whole atmosphere is so darkened that they find it hard to advance. Nevertheless this is also God's preparation for the rapture of the overcomers.

We need to understand what soul power is and what this force of the soul can do. Let me say that before the Lord's return similar things to these will be greatly increased, perhaps even more than a hundredfold. Satan will perform many astonishing feats by utilizing this soul power so as to deceive God's elect.

We are now drawing nearer to the time of great apostasy. "The momentum is increasing rapidly," observed Mrs. Penn-Lewis. "The hand of the Archenemy of God and man is on the helm, and the world is rushing to the dark hour, when, for a brief period, Satan will actually be the 'god of this age', ruling through a superman whose 'parousia' (appearance) cannot long be delayed."* What is soul power? By

---

*Penn-Lewis, *op. cit.*, p.69.

going to the Scriptures and under the illumination of the Holy Spirit believers ought to realize that this power is so hellish as to spread over all nations on earth and to turn the whole world into chaos.

Satan is now engaging this soul power to serve as a substitute for God's gospel and its power. He tries to blind people's hearts, through the marvel of soul force, into accepting a bloodless religion. He also uses the discoveries of psychic sciences to cast doubt upon the value of supernatural occurrences in Christianity—causing people to consider the latter as likewise being nothing but the latent power of the soul. He aims at substituting Christ's salvation with psychic force. The modern attempt to change evil habits and bad temperaments by hypnosis is a forerunner to this objective.

The children of God can be protected only by knowing the difference between spirit and soul. If the deeper work of the cross is not applied to our Adamic life and by the Holy Spirit a real life union is effected with the Resurrected Lord, we may unwittingly develop our soul power.

It may be helpful here to quote again from Mrs. Penn-Lewis.

'Soul-force' versus 'Spirit-force' is the battleground today. The Body of Christ is by the energy of the Holy Spirit within her, advancing heavenward. The atmosphere of the world is thickening with psychic currents behind which are massed the aerial foes. The only safety for the child of God is an experimental knowledge of the life in union with Christ wherein he dwells with Christ in God, above the poisonous air in which the prince of the power of the air carries on his work. The Blood of Christ for cleansing. The Cross of Christ for identification in death. The Power of the Risen Ascended Lord by the Holy Ghost, continually declared, laid hold of and wielded, will alone bring the members of the Body through in victory to join the Ascended Head.*

My hope for today is that you may be helped to know the source and the operations of the latent power of the soul. May God impress us with the fact that where soul force is, there also is the evil spirit. We must not use the power which comes from us, rather must we use the power which proceeds from the Holy Spirit. May we especially deny the latent power of the soul, lest we fall into Satan's hand. For the soul's power has, through Adam's sin, already fallen under the dominion of Satan and has become the latter's working instrument. We therefore need to exercise great caution against Satan's deception.

---

*Penn-Lewis, *op. cit.*, p.70.

2 The Christian and Psychic Force

We have already seen how Adam was endued with unusual and astonishing abilities when he was created by God. These seemingly miraculous powers fell together with Adam. People who are ignorant tend to think that at his fall Adam lost all of his wonderful powers. But the evidences produced by modern parapsychology indicate that Adam had not lost his original power, only that he had it hidden in his soul. During the past five or six thousand years, there have been quite a few among unbelievers who were able to demonstrate this soul force. Within the last one hundred years, more and more people are capable of manifesting this latent power of the soul. Adam's original ability has not been lost, it is merely hidden away in his flesh. In this portion of the message I will speak on the relation between this latent psychic power and a Christian. Unless we know its danger we will not know how to guard against it. I invite you to observe especially the following four facts.

Four Facts

(1) There is in Adam an almost unlimited power, a near miraculous ability. This we call soul power. Modern psychic researchers have proved the existence of such ability within man. Since the discovery of Mesmer in 1778 all kinds of latent power have been exhibited—whether expressed psychically or religiously. These are but the release of man's soul force. We should not forget that these powers of the soul were in man before his fall but became latent in him afterwards.

(2) Satan desires to control man's latent soul power. He is well aware that there is this power in man's soul which is capable of doing many things. He therefore wishes to bring it under his control instead of God's. Satan wants to use it for his own purpose. The purpose of his tempting Adam and Eve in the garden was to gain control of their soul power.

I have frequently spoken on the spiritual meanings of the tree of the knowledge of good and evil and the tree of life. The meaning of the tree of the knowledge of good and evil is *in*dependence, the taking of independent action. The tree of life, though, signifies *de*pendence or reliance on God. The significance of this tree further tells us that Adam's original life is but a human life, and that therefore he needs to depend on God and receive God's life in order to live. But the tree of the knowledge of good and evil discloses that man does not need to depend on God but he can work and live and bear fruit all by himself. Why do I bring up these matters? Simply to show you the cause of Adam and Eve's fall. If we can release Adam's latent power we too may work wonders. But are we permitted to do so?

Satan knew there was such wonder-working strength in man, hence he tempted man to declare his independence from God. The fall in the Edenic garden was none other than man taking independent action, separating himself from God. Upon learning the story of the fall in the garden, we can perceive what the purpose of Satan was. He aimed at gaining the soul of man. And when man fell, his original ability and miraculous strength all fell into Satan's hand.

(3) Today Satan desires to release and display the latent power of the soul. As soon as man fell, God imprisoned man's psychic powers in his flesh. His many powers became confined and hidden in the flesh as a latent force—present but inactive. After the fall, all which belongs to the soul comes under the control and bondage of that which belongs to the flesh. All psychological forces are thus governed by physiological forces. Satan's objective is to liberate man's soul power through the breakdown of the outer shell of his flesh so as to free his soul from its fleshly bonds, thereby manifesting his latent power. This is what Revelation 18.13 means by making mer-

chandise of men's souls. Indeed, man's soul has become one of the many items of the enemy's commodities. The enemy desires especially to have man's psychological abilities as his merchandise.

At the end of the age, particularly during the present moment, Satan's intention is to carry through what he at the beginning aimed at in the garden of Eden. Although he initiated the work of controlling man's soul in the garden, he had not fully succeeded. For after his fall, man's whole being, including his soul power, came under the flesh. In other words, man's psychological forces came under the dominion of his physiological forces. The enemy failed to make use of man's soul power; accordingly his plan was foiled.

Throughout these thousands of years, Satan has been exerting himself to influence men into expressing their latent power. He has found, now and then, here and there, persons from whom he succeeds in drawing out their soul force. These have become wonder-working religious leaders of the ages. But in the last hundred years, since the discovery of Mesmer in parapsychology, many new discoveries of psychic phenomena have followed. All these are due to but one reason: the enemy is attempting to finish his previously unsuccessful work. He intends to release all the latent powers of men. This is his singular purpose which he has been cultivating for thousands of years. This is why he trades in the souls of men besides such merchandise as gold, silver, precious stones, pearls, and cattle and horses. As a matter of fact, he has exerted his utmost strength to obtain this special commodity.

(4) How does Satan make use of these latent powers? What are the various advantages for him?

(a) He will be able to fulfill his original promise he made to man that "ye shall be as God". In their ability to work so many wonders, men will consider themselves as gods, and worship not God but themselves.

(b) He will confuse God's miracles. He wishes mankind to believe that all the miracles in the Bible are but psychological in their origin, thus lowering their value. He wants men to think that they are able to do whatever the Lord Jesus did.

(c) He will confound the work of the Holy Spirit. The Holy Spirit works in man through the human spirit, but now Satan forges in man's soul many phenomena similar to the workings of the Holy Spirit, causing man to experience false repentance, false salvation, false regeneration, false revival, false joy, and other counterfeits of Holy Spirit experiences.

(d) He will use man as his instrument for his final resistance against God's plan in this last age. The Holy Spirit is God's miracle-working power; but man's soul is Satan's wonder-working power. The last three years and a half (during the great tribulation) will be a period of great wonders performed by man's soul under Satan's direction.

In summary, then, we see that (1) all these miraculous powers are already in Adam, (2) Satan's objective is to control these powers, (3) in the end time

Satan is, and will continue to be, especially engaged in manifesting these powers, and (4) this is his attempt to finish his earlier unsuccessful task.

The Point of Difference in the Workings of God and Satan

How should we guard against deception? We need to discern what is God's operation and what is the enemy's operation, what work is done by the Holy Spirit and what work is done by the evil spirit. All the works of the Holy Spirit are done through man's spirit; but the works of the enemy are all done through man's soul. The Holy Spirit moves the human spirit while the enemy spirit moves the human soul. This is the basic point of difference between the operations of God and those of the enemy. God's work is initiated by the Holy Spirit, but the enemy's work is commenced in man's soul.

Because of the fall, our human spirit is dead and so cannot communicate with God. At the time we believe in the Lord Jesus we are born again. What is meant by being saved or born again? This is not just a matter of terminology; a real organic change has occurred in us. When we trust in the Lord Jesus, God puts His life into our spirit and quickens it. Just as man's spirit is substantial, so too this new spirit which God puts in us is substantial.

John 3.6 tells us what new birth is. "That which is born of the Spirit is spirit." Ezekiel too informs us:

"A new spirit will I (God) put within you" (36.26). Hence in regeneration we get a new spirit. On one occasion the Lord Jesus said: "The words that I have spoken unto you are spirit, and are life" (John 6.63). Our life and work must therefore all be within the scope of the spirit. When God uses us He usually works in and through our spirit. "Be filled with the Spirit" (Eph. 5.18) indicates that this new spirit of ours should be filled with the Holy Spirit. In other words, God fills our spirit with His Holy Spirit.

The Holy Spirit works in our spirit; but the evil spirit operates in our soul. Satan can only operate in the soul and by the power of the soul. Satan has no way to commence his work in man's spirit; his working is restricted to the soul. What he has been doing for the past five or six thousand years he is presently doing and will continue to do in the future. Why is it that Satan seems to be as omnipotent, omnipresent, and omniscient as God? For no other reason than what he is able to do with man's soul power. We may say that while the Holy Spirit is the power of God, man's soul appears to be the power of Satan.

How unfortunate that many people are ignorant of the fact that the many ascetic practices, breathings, and abstract meditations of Buddhism and Taoism, the hypnotism of western Europe, and the numerous wonders seen in psychic researches are only the manifestations of the latent power of man's soul. They do not realize how mighty is the power of the soul.

Brothers and sisters, let us not consider this as a

minor problem nor dismiss it as a research for scholars. It actually has profound effects upon us.

The Two Sides of Soul Power

According to the Bible, the latent power of the soul seems to include two types. This parallels the classification seen from the psychological standpoint. We confess that we are unable to divide these two types neatly; all we can say is that there seems to be two different types in the soul's latent power: one seems to be the ordinary kind while the other seems to be the miraculous kind; one seems to be natural, the other seems to be supernatural; one seems to be humanly comprehensible, the other seems to be beyond human comprehension.

The term "mind" in psychology is broader in its meaning than that used in the Bible. What the psychologists mean by the "mind" or the "heart" includes two parts: consciousness and subconsciousness. The subconscious side is what we call the miraculous part of the power of the soul. Though psychologists make the distinction between consciousness and subconsciousness, they can hardly separate them. They only classify the more common psychical manifestations as belonging to the first type—that of consciousness, whereas they group the extraordinary or miraculous manifestations under the second category—that of subconsciousness. We usually include only those common manifestations within the scope of the soul, not knowing that the strange and miraculous manifestation is also of the soul, though manifestations of this type are more in the realm of the subconscious. Owing to various degrees of latent power in individual souls, some men exhibit phenomena more within the first type; while others, more within the second type.

All who serve the Lord ought to pay special attention to this point, otherwise they will get carried away by miraculous powers while trying to help people. Let me reiterate the difference between soul and spirit: Adam's fallen soul belongs to the old creation; but the regenerated spirit is the new creation. God works with man's spirit, for this is his regenerated life, his new creation. Satan, on the other hand, builds with man's soul—that is, the fallen soul in Adam. He can only use the old creation because the regenerated life in the new creation does not sin.

What Satan Is Doing in the Church Today

How does Satan operate through man's soul and work with its latent psychical power? We have already given many examples in Buddhism, Taoism, Christianity, parapsychology, and so forth. Let us now illustrate with some instances showing how Satan will use man's soul in spiritual things. This will help the Christian to discern what is of God and what is of the enemy, and also to know how God uses man's spirit whereas Satan uses man's soul.

Prayer

The prayers in the Bible are intelligent and not silly. When the Lord Jesus teaches us to pray, His first words are: "Our Father who art in heaven". He teaches us to pray to our Father in heaven, but we Christians often pray to the God in our room. Our prayer should be offered to the heavenly Father for Him to hear. God wants us to send our prayers to heaven by faith, regardless if our feeling be good or bad, or even if there be no feeling. If you pray to, and expect to be heard by, the God in your room, I am afraid you will receive many strange feelings and miraculous experiences and visions from the God in your room. These are given to you by Satan, and whatever you receive from Satan belongs either to consciousness or subconsciousness.

Someone may not pray to the God in his room. He may direct his prayers instead towards the person for whom he prays. This too is most dangerous. Suppose you have a friend who is over two thousand miles away from you. You pray for him, asking God, as the case might be, to either revive him in the Word or to save him. Instead of directing your prayer towards God, you concentrate on your thought, your expectation, and your wish and send them out to your friend as a force. Your prayer is like a bow which shoots your thought, desire and wish as arrows towards your friend. He will be so oppressed by this force that he will do exactly what you have asked for. You may think your prayer is answered. But let me tell you, it is not God who answers your prayer, for you have not prayed to Him. It is merely an answer to a prayer which you directed towards your friend.

Someone claims his prayer is answered because, says he, "I have piled prayers on my friend." Indeed, for you prayed towards *him*, not towards God. Your prayer is answered, but not by God. Even though you do not know hypnosis, what you have secretly done has fulfilled the law of hypnotism. You have released your psychic force to perform this act.

Why is this so? Because you have not prayed to the God in heaven; instead your prayers are projected towards, piled upon, and laid seige to, the person for whom you pray. In appearance you are praying, but in actuality you are oppressing that person with your psychic power. If you use your soul force in praying for a certain one—say you pray that he should be at least disciplined if not punished—the prayer of your soul force will dart out at him and he will accordingly be sick. This is a fixed principle of the soul. It is as sure as the fact that a person will be scorched if he thrusts his finger into fire.

For this reason, we should not pray a prayer that asks that a person be punished if he does not do what is expected of him. Such prayer will cause him to suffer, and thus make the one who prayed such a prayer the instigator of his woe. If we pray, we should pray to God and not towards man. I personally have experienced the ill-effect of such prayer. Several years ago I was sick for over a year. This was due to the prayers of five or six persons being piled upon me. The more they prayed, the weaker I became. Finally I discovered the cause. I began to resist such prayers, asking God to disengage me from what they had prayed for. And so I got well. In this connection, let me quote from a letter written by a believer:

> I have just come through a terrible onslaught of the enemy. Hemorrhage, heart affection, panting and exhaustion. My whole body is in a state of collapse. It suddenly burst upon me while at prayer to pray against all psychic power exercised upon me by (psychic) 'prayer'. By faith in the power of the Blood of Christ, I cut myself off from it, and the result was remarkable. Instantly my breathing became normal, the hemorrhage stopped, exhaustion vanished, all pain fled, and life came back into my body. I have been refreshed and invigorated ever since. God let me know in confirmation of this deliverance, that my condition was the effect of a group of deceived souls, who are in opposition to me, 'praying' about me! God had used me to the deliverance of two of them, but the rest are in an awful pit . . . .*

Power for Service

If one who is experienced in the Lord is present at a revival meeting, he can tell whether the speaker is

---

*Mrs. Jessie Penn-Lewis, *Soul and Spirit.* Poole, Dorset, Eng-

using soulical or spiritual power. Once a friend of mine told me how powerful a certain preacher was. As I had never before met this preacher, I said I dare not judge. But I did write a few words on a notebook and gave it to my friend. I wrote: "Full of power but what power?" This friend was not as advanced in the Lord as was his wife. He did not understand what I had written. So he turned to ask his wife. After reading the note, she laughingly admitted, "This is indeed a real problem. What power is that preacher filled with?" Once a brother among us observed that whether someone had power or not could not be judged by how hard he was able to pound the pulpit. We need to discern in a meeting if a person's power is psychical or spiritual.

We may judge this power from two directions: from the preacher himself and from the audience. If a preacher relies on his past experience—wherein people repented through a message he gave—by deciding to deliver a message a second time with the expectation of getting the same result as at the first, he is undoubtedly working with his psychic power. Or if he tries to stir up people by relating many stories of repentance, he again will be using his psychic power.

On the other hand, if the attitude of a preacher is like that of Evan Roberts, God's vessel in the Welsh Revival of 1904-5, then his soul power will be denied.

---

land, Overcomer Literature Trust, 1968?, p.58. Also available in the United States from Christian Literature Crusade, Fort Washington, Pa.

For that servant of the Lord asked God to bend him, to bind his soul power, to bridle his self, and to block all which came out of him. He who ministers ought to know the difference between these two forces. He should be able to discern what is done by his soul power and what is done by the power of God.

The work of the Holy Spirit is threefold: (1) to regenerate us, (2) to indwell us that we may produce the fruit of the Spirit, and (3) to come upon us that we may have the power to witness. Now whenever the Bible touches on the power of the Holy Spirit, it invariably points to work or witnessing. This refers to the Holy Spirit coming upon us, not to His working within us. It is clear that the power of the Holy Spirit is for work; the indwelling is for fruit. The power of the Holy Spirit is always spoken of in the original text of the Bible as descending or coming upon, while the fruit-bearing aspect of the Holy Spirit is spoken of as abiding in.

Why is the enabling power of the Holy Spirit spoken of as being upon? Because the enabling which the Holy Spirit gives you is outside of you. You cannot be sure of it. Therefore if in a meeting people ask you whether you are confident of today's meeting—confident that people will be saved—you have to confess that you have no assurance whatsoever. For this power is exterior to you. The power of the Holy Spirit is beyond your control. But if this is soul force, you are assured of it. You know your message can cause people to weep and to make them repent. What is called dynamic power is merely the power of the soul.

Once I felt powerless. Although other people told me I was satisfactory, I felt rather feeble. So I went to see an elderly experienced sister, Margaret E. Barber. I said to her, "Your power is great, why do I not have power?" We knew each other well, and she frequently helped me in spiritual matters. She looked at me seriously and asked, "What power do you want—what you may feel or what you cannot feel?" As soon as I heard, I understood. I therefore answered, "I want what I cannot feel." So she said, "You must remember that there is no need for people to feel the power which comes from the Holy Spirit. Man's duty is to obey God. For the power of the Holy Spirit is not given for man to feel." (Note that sensing in the spirit is another matter.) My duty is to ask God to bind my soul force, that is, my own power. I am to obey God absolutely, the rest I leave to Him to do.

If we work with soul force, we can feel it just as do the hypnotists, who know what results they will get by doing certain things. They know from the first step to the last step. The peril of the pulpit lies in the fact that many preachers do not know they are using their own psychic force. They think they have power; but they are only employing psychological power to win people.

Some have suggested that preachers have become experts on the use of psychology in manipulating people. But I strongly repudiate such manipulation; for even though we know how to attract people with psychic means, we should purposely avoid using any psychic force. Once I was working in Shantung. A professor there said to his colleague "that these preachers work with emotions." It so happened that when I preached to the believers that afternoon I told them how undependable and useless was emotion. The colleague professor who was told by the first professor that preachers use emotion was also present at the meeting. After he heard my word he said it was a pity that the professor who spoke to him was absent.

Let us remember that all works done through emotion are questionable and transient. In the work done through the power of the Holy Spirit man does not need to exert his own strength nor do anything by himself. If a work is done by soul strength one has to exert lots of energy and employ numerous methods such as weeping, shouting, jumping, incessant singing of choruses, or the telling of a number of moving stories (I do not say that hymns and stories should not be used, only everything must be done within appropriate bounds). For the employment of these methods serves no other purpose than that of trying to stir up the audience.

We all know that some individuals have a magnetic attraction about them. Though they may not be fairer or more eloquent than others, they nonetheless can draw people to themselves. Often have people told me, "You have great influence over So-and-so, why do you not pull him over?" To which I answer, "That is useless." For this will merely be natural; it is not spiritual at all. Many mistake Christianity to be a kind of psychic phenomenon as though it belongs to the domain of psychology. We really cannot blame them, because we believers make the mistake first. Unless the power of God draws your parents or your children, your natural attraction—however great it may be—is of no avail. Even if you could draw them with your dynamic force, what, if anything, is really gained?

Peace and Joy

What is the highest attainment in Christianity? That of complete union with God and total loss of self. In modern psychology there is also the so-called union of man with the invisible "mind" so as to cause him to lose his identity. This appears to be akin to Christianity, though in reality these two are far apart. The popular Dr. Frank Buchman (Oxford Group movement) advocated this kind of psychology. One of his teachings concerned meditation. He reckoned that meditation was all that was necessary for communication between man and God. He did not ask people to read the Bible at early morn; he only asked them to meditate and then to pray. The first thought which comes after prayer, he proclaimed, is that thought which is given you by God. And so you must live through the day according to that thought. Who would ever think that this is but another type of silent sitting or abstract meditation? What is the effect of such meditation? You will be told that it will make you most peaceful and joyous. If you quietly direct your thought on whatever thing it may be for an hour, you too will get what is called peace and joy. Even if you meditate abstractly for one hour on no thought at all, you will still not fail to obtain this so-called peace and joy.

The meditations of many people are simply a kind of psychic operation. Not so with the Christian faith. We need not meditate on God, for we already have God's life. We can know Him in our intuition, regardless what our feeling may be. We have within us an intuitive guidance to the knowledge of God. In addition we have the word of God. Whatever His word says, we believe. If we have faith, we can disregard feeling. Herein lie the differences between Christian faith and psychology.

Wonders

Let us look at wonders. I personally am not antagonistic to them. I have seen with my own eyes cases of instantaneous divine healing. Some people profess they can heal diseases. We do not oppose healing, we only contend with erroneous ways of healing. Some ask me if I oppose speaking in tongues. Certainly not, though I do question tongues which are obtained through faulty means. As to visions and dreams, I too have seen great light. We acknowledge that there are such things in the Bible. But I do resist visions and dreams which are obtained through unlawful means.

The Bible speaks of the laying on of hands and the anointing with oil. Some, however, in laying hands on another's head, rub forcibly the back of the person's brain or his neck and keep on asking how that person feels. Naturally when he is massaged, his neck will feel heated up. This is such a low trick that even the hypnotists reject using it. We know that at the back of our brain is a big nerve which extends into the vertebrae. The one who massages may not realize that this is a kind of hypnosis. The one who is being massaged may sense a current of warmth passing through his vertebrae and may even be healed. Yet it is but the manifestation of the latent psychical power of man. In spite of his getting well, I cannot recognize it as *divine* healing.

Spirit-Baptism

Let us talk about the baptism in the Holy Spirit. When I was in Shantung this time, I too told people to seek for it. Nevertheless, I do not approve of the shutting in of many people into a small room for several days' fasting, praying, and chorus singing. Should people do such a thing, it will not take too long for them to have their brain dazed, the will to be turned passive, and their lips to be made to utter strange and incoherent sounds or tongues. And in this way shall their latent power be released.

In a meeting for seeking Spirit-baptism, people will keep shouting hallelujah for thousands of times.

Eventually, their brain will grow dull, their mind becomes paralyzed, and they begin to see visions. How can you consider this as Spirit-baptism? It is but soul-baptism. What they receive is not the power of the Holy Spirit; it is instead soul force, the manifestation of the latent power of the soul. It comes from human exercise, not from the enduement of God. This is not the proper way for seeking the baptism in the Holy Spirit. Yet people are still coaching others in this way, a way they learn not at God's instruction but by their own past experiences.

Some may ask, after reading this, "According to what you say, is it true that there are no real miracles?" Of course there are. We give thanks to God for all the miracles which come from Him. Nonetheless, we need to discern that if a miracle does not come from God, it is performed by the latent psychical power of man. When I was in Shantung I heard of a woman, palsied for many years, being completely healed. If her healing was truly of God, I would thank Him for her.

Knowing Psychic Force

Mrs. Mary Baker Eddy, founder of the Church of Christ, Scientist, denied that there were death, sickness and pain; yet she died. However, the Church of Christ, Scientist outlives her and continues on prosperously. They still give assent to the notion that if a sick person believes he is not sick, he will feel no pain; if a dying person believes he will not die, he will not die. As a consequence, many people are healed. Their propagators merely try to strengthen man's psychic force for the relief of physical ailment. Through the release of man's latent power of the soul, bodily weakness is overcome.

Because of the development of the soul's latent force, wonders are increasing nowadays. Of these wonders, many are highly supernatural and miraculous. Yet all these are only the manifestations of the latent power of the soul. Though I am no prophet, I have read books on prophecy. I learn that hereafter soul's latent power will have greater manifestations. For in the last days the enemy will seize upon man's psychic force to fulfill his work. If he succeeds in seizing this power, he will be able to do great wonders.

There are two classes of people who hold to two extremes respectively. One class insists there is no wonder. When they hear about wonders such as divine healing, they refuse to listen. Another class lays stress on wonders so much that they do not care from what source come these wonders—from God or from the enemy. Today we should be careful not to bend to either extreme. Each time we see or hear of a wonder performed we must ask, Is this God's doing or the enemy's? Is it done by the Holy Spirit of God or by the law of human psychology?

Today we should use our abilities—such as that of the mind, the will and the emotion—to do things, but we ought not express the latent power that is in our soul. The mind, emotion and will are man's psychic organs which he cannot help but use. For if *man* does not use them the evil spirit will take over their usage. However, if man desires to use *the latent power behind* these abilities, the evil spirit will begin to give him all kinds of counterfeit miracles. All works done by the soul and its psychic law are counterfeits. Only what is done by the power of the Holy Spirit is real. The Holy Spirit has His own law of operation. For it is stated in Romans 8.2, "the law of the Spirit of life". Thank God, the Holy Spirit is real, and the law of the Holy Spirit is factual. Wonders performed according to the law of the Holy Spirit come from God.

It is extremely difficult for Moslems to believe in the Lord Jesus. There are therefore comparatively few who become Christians. Now how do the Moslems pray? Three times every day they do so in their mosques. They say that if anything needs to be done, pray in one accord with tens of thousands of people. "Consider the mass of Mahomedans at prayer in the great Jumna Mosque of Delhi," writes Mrs. Penn-Lewis, "where an hundred thousand followers of Mahomet assemble inside the Mosque, with a still larger crowd engaged in prayer outside." For what were they praying? In unison they shouted that they wanted Turkey revived and freed from the domination of the white race. Their psychic force gained the victory. "It is sufficient," continues Mrs. Penn-Lewis, "to point to the revision of the Treaty of Sevres, under which all that was lost to Turkey had to be restored. A greater triumph of one Eastern nation over all Western nations put together, cannot be imagined. The explanation given, and believed in by millions in India, is expressed in the word 'soul-force'."* Unfortunately the prayers of many Christians are not answered by God but are attained by the projection of the latent power of their soul. They accomplish their goals in much the same way as the Moslems.

Look now at the powers displayed in Hinduism. Some Hindus can walk on fire without being scorched. And this is not a fake. They walk on fire, and not just a few steps, but across a long course with their feet treading on red-hot iron; yet they are not hurt. Some of them can lie on beds with nails pointed up. (Naturally, those whom they consider beginners cannot bear such things and will feel pain and hurt.) This too is a matter of the development of psychic power. How disastrous for believers to perform wonders with the same power which the Hindus use.

Very often in meetings Christians can sense a sort of power pressing in on them, or even at times of prayer and Bible reading they may feel oppressed without any reason. All these come from Satan who uses psychic forces to depress us or to assault us. Experienced Christians all over the world are aware of the especially severe attacks of the enemy at the end of this age. Since the whole atmosphere of the world

---

*Mrs. Jessie Penn-Lewis, *Spirit and Soul.* Poole, Dorset, England, Overcomer Literature Trust, 1968?, p.56. Also available in the United States from Christian Literature Crusade, Fort Washington, Pa.

seems to be heavily charged with psychic force, we need to hide ourselves under the Lord's precious blood and be protected by it.

While listening to a sermon in a huge cathedral, you can sense almost instantly if soul power is in operation—whether there is something present which seems to be inciting you. Although the preacher may announce that some people have repented and have been saved, you need to consider the consequences for those proclaimed to be saved. For there has been the mixing in of improper power into the work. If the power has come from God—which is that of God's Spirit—you would have felt light and clear. But psychic force as used by the enemy is aroused by the presence of a big crowd. May we be able to discern the difference lest we too be deceived.

The time is now come. Satan is exciting all his energies and using all kinds of means to stir up the latent power of the soul in religionists, mental scientists, and even Christians. Such is the fact before us. We should ask the Lord to give us light that we may discern.

3 Spirit Force vs. Psychic Force

We will continue with this important topic of the latent power of the soul. We have seen what psychic force can do and have heard how to distinguish between things of God and things not of God. At the end of this age there are many wonders, miracles and supernatural feats. Are these performed by God Himself or by the operation of another kind of power? We need to know how to divide the spiritual from the soulical. We will now relate still further how soul power works; that is, what its operational methods are. Such knowledge will further help us to know what is of God and what is not of God.

Prophecies in the Bible

But first, let us look into the Scriptures to discover what are the signs at the end of this age and before the imminent return of the Lord.

> For there shall arise false Christs, and false prophets, and shall show great signs and wonders; so as to lead astray, if possible, even the elect. (Matt. 24.24)
>
> And the beast which I saw was like unto a leopard, and his feet were as the feet of a bear, and his mouth as the mouth of a lion: and the dragon gave him his power, and his throne, and great authority. And I saw one of his heads as though it had been smitten unto death; and his death-stroke was healed: and the whole earth wondered after the beast; and they worshipped the dragon, because he gave his authority unto the beast...and there was given to him authority to continue forty and two months...And he exerciseth all the authority of the first beast in his sight. And he maketh the earth and them that dwell therein to worship the first beast, whose death-stroke was healed. And he doeth great signs, that he should even make fire to come down out of heaven upon the earth in the sight of man. (Rev. 13.2-5,12-13)
>
> And then shall be revealed the lawless one, whom the Lord Jesus shall slay with the breath of his mouth, and bring to nought by the manifestation of his coming; even he, whose coming is according to the working of Satan with all power and signs and lying wonders, and with all deceit of unrighteousness for them that perish; because they received not the love of the truth, that they might be saved. (2 Thess. 2.8-10)

Before we explain these passages please notice that in 2 Thessalonians 2.9 there are said to be "lying wonders"—wonders are actually performed, but with the objective of deceiving the people. These phenomena are not imaginings but facts. Only, their motive is deceptive.

All three passages we have just read point to one matter: these are things that will transpire in the great tribulation. Yet without a doubt some of these occurrences seem to happen before the time of the great tribulation. This is in accordance with a rather obvious rule in the Bible—that before the fulfillment of a prophecy there usually occurs beforehand something similar which stands as a foretoken of its final realization. For this reason many prophetic scholars agree that things which will come to pass during the great tribulation are now happening one after another, though not as intense as will be the case in the future days.

Now the Bible passages which we have quoted above have already shown us the characteristic of the great tribulation period. During that time there will be great signs and wonders. Before the coming of the Lord, what the Antichrist will be particularly interested in performing are signs and wonders. It is common knowledge that before a person arrives, his shadow is first seen, and his voice is heard ahead of him. Likewise, before the arrival of the great tribulation, the shadow and sound of the signs and wonders of the great tribulation are already present. Since signs and wonders will become most common during the great tribulation, these are bound to increase in our present day.

A Personal Remark

Before we proceed further, I would like to make a remark. I personally am not antagonistic to miracles. There are many recorded in the Bible; and they are most precious and extremely important. I have stressed in the past how a believer needs to grow in several respects. Let me reiterate them once again. First, after one is saved he should seek for proper knowledge of the Bible. Second, he should desire to make progress in the spiritual life, such as victory, holiness, perfect love, and so forth. This is very very important. Third, we should be fervent in winning souls. Fourth, we should trust in God with such singleness of faith that we may see God working miracles.

There are many defects in the church today. Many believers are interested in nothing more than the expounding of the Scriptures. Their knowledge is excellent, yet they neither care for nor seek after growth in spiritual life. Or some may go a step further and search for the higher life and the deeper things of God, but they neglect the other three aspects. Still others have zeal but have no knowledge. All such lopsided strivings are unhealthy. Is it not surprising that in the church today those who seek to either literally or spiritually expound the Bible, or to pursue after deeper and richer life, or to be zealous in soul winning are not lacking in number, but few there be who trust God with a living faith so as to obtain something from Him?

Every believer should strive to develop equally these four aspects of growth so that there be no unbalanced situation. Miracles, therefore, I am not against. On the contrary, I value them highly. I nonetheless call for discernment due to false miracles and lying wonders. Hence when I speak about these counterfeits I have not the slightest thought of opposing miracles per se.

Please remember that all the works of God are done by the Holy Spirit with the cooperation of our spirit. They are never realized by man's soul. It is Satan who makes use of the power of man's soul—that psychic force which due to the fall is now hidden in man's flesh. And it is therefore inevitable that in the last days he will raise up an Antichrist who will be given his own power and authority, for he will have to rely upon the latent power of man's soul.

I will now give some examples to help us in understanding how certain phenomena are not the demonstrations of spiritual power but are the manifestations of soul's latent force. Since we have already dealt with the miraculous side of the soul's power, we will here focus on its non-miraculous side.

Example 1 — *Personal Evangelism*

Just as our psychological conditions vary from

one person to another so our soul powers differ too. Some people have stronger minds; they can sometimes read others' thoughts. One may think that in order to find appropriate words with which to talk to another person he must know the thought of that person. This is the natural way of knowing, which should be rejected.

Forgive me for illustrating this point out of my own personal experience. In my contact with people I can easily ascertain their thoughts after only a short exchange of words. I just know without any special reason. When I first began to serve the Lord I thought such natural perception of the other's mind was most helpful in the work. But upon understanding better, I dared not use my natural ability further. Each time such a situation arises now, I immediately resist with prayer.

In talking with people, it is not necessary for you to know what they are thinking about in their minds. Furthermore, it is vain; for whatever is of the soul and done by its power will end in vanity. If a work is done by psychic force it will not build up another person's life even though he may profess to be helped, because there is no real profit deposited in the depth of his being. So when an individual comes to you, the most important thing for you to do is to ask God to show you how to help him. You should tell the Lord that, as you do not know what that man is thinking about nor are certain of his psychic and spiritual condition, you come to Him in utter dependence for Him to give you appropriate words.

What you need is to lay down yourself completely in order to receive help from God.

Example 2 — *Revival Meeting*

It is rather amazing how many brothers who preach a lot mention the matter of meetings to me. They assert that if they go to a church hall and find the lights dim, attendance low, and empty chairs abundant, they seem to lose their power upon standing up to preach. But should the lights be burning bright and the audience full and enthusiastic, they appear to grow in power. But what kind of power is this?

May I frankly say that this is none other than the power of your own soul force. The power which comes from the Holy Spirit is never affected by outside environment. Anyone who wishes to know what preaching in soul power is need only attend a big meeting packed with people and provided with the finest equipment, and just listen to the people singing and watch the movement of the audience. You will be able to sense that there is special power in a crowded place. What power is this? Do you feel a force which presses on you? It cannot be the power of the Holy Spirit. It is the power of the soul.

Why is it considered soul power? Just observe what these people are doing. In singing, they sing in unison towards one direction, resulting in the concentration of all the soul powers generated by the multi-

tude. How great is this power! You may come with
the thought of helping them, but in such an atmosphere you will instead be influenced by them. How
dangerous this is. A great many of the Lord's servants
tell me the same story as to how the numbers in
attendance or the atmosphere of the gathering and so
forth will either help or hinder their work. I always
answer that they are controlled by circumstance because they preach in their own strength.

Example 3 — *Singing*

Many times singing is of great assistance in God's
work. Sometimes, though, it cannot help but be a
soulical activity. A great number of people enjoy
visiting certain church groups because the music there
is superb. Some groups spend over a million dollars
merely to install a pipe organ. We have heard people
say that when they go to such places, the moment
they hear the sound of the organ and the voice of
singing their spirits are immediately released to God's
presence. Indeed, such a thing does happen. But are
they really being brought to the presence of God?
Can people's spirits be released and drawn closer to
God by a little attraction such as this? Is this God's
way?

I am afraid many arrangements in these places are
carnal. They try to stir up a man's emotion and incite
his religious instinct through the sounds of organ and
song. Such power is not of God, but of hymns and

music. We too sing hymns, but we will not put our confidence in hymns. Only what is done by the Holy Spirit is profitable; nothing else can reach into our spirit.

Have you ever been to a remote country place? Thank God, He gave me the opportunity to visit such a place. Once I went to a village by the sea. The inhabitants there were all fishermen. There were believers scattered throughout the vicinity of this village. They had meetings with sometimes twenty, thirty, or even fifty or sixty persons present. Whenever they all assemble together and sing, what an irregular tune pierces your ears! Some sing fast and some sing slow, resulting in a lapse of several minutes because the fast ones have already finished the last line but must wait for a spell until the slower ones catch up. Can you possibly meet under this kind of circumstance? You will probably be dying with impatience, and your power will be all but dissipated. One brother told me that after listening to their singing he could no longer preach. I answered him by saying that there was a reason for it: Did the power come from him or from God?

You and I usually look to the environment and are influenced by it. But if it is of the Holy Spirit, we will be controlling the environment. This is a deep principle to which each of us should hold fast. Let us not use our own psychic force lest we be controlled by environment.

Sometimes in an oppressive atmosphere singing may be used by God to release people. Prayer at times may too be a help. But if we make singing or prayer the center, we face the peril of releasing soul power. Many people live carelessly for six days, and then attend a church meeting on Sunday. They hear the singing of many hymns and feel warm and joyful. But let us inquire from whence this kind of warmth and joy comes? I can prove that something is defective here. Should a person live casually for six days and then come to God one day, he should instead feel guilty and reprove himself. How then is it that the singing makes him feel warm and joyful? This cannot be spiritual power. I do not wish to be a narrow critic, but it must be pointed out that too much singing does excite soul power.

Example 4 — *Bible Expounding*

There is the danger of expressing the latent power of the soul even in studying the Bible. For instance, someone is puzzled over a certain passage of Scripture. He does not understand what it means. So he constantly thinks about it, whether walking on the road or sleeping in his bed or sitting in his study or riding on the train. Suddenly a flash of light shines on him; he now seems to be able to expound that passage to himself logically. If he has a good memory he will no doubt store it in his mind; if his memory is not so keen he will write it down in a notebook. Is not such a sudden interpretation wonderful? Yet the question must be asked, Is this dependable? Because it can sometimes come from soul power. By looking at its result, the interpretation can be fairly judged. For such novel, special, seemingly profound exposition may not bear spiritual fruit. Not only he himself may not derive life from it, he may also have no way to impart life to others while giving out his interpretation. All he can do is to help the mind of people a little.

Example 5—*Joy*

A great number of people desire to have joy in their feeling. The so-called holy laugh is an extreme case in point. It is taught that if a person is filled with the Holy Spirit he invariably will have this holy laugh. He who claims to have this kind of laughing cannot control himself. Without any reason he will laugh and laugh and laugh as if infected by a certain disease, and will appear to be partially insane.

Once in a certain meeting, after the sermon was concluded, it was announced that everybody should seek for this holy laugh. All began to beat tables or chairs, jumping and leaping all around, until not long afterwards this so-called holy laughing came. People would merely look at one another and break out laughing. The more they thought about it the funnier it became. And so they could not contain themselves and kept on laughing. What is this? Can this possibly be the fullness of the Holy Spirit? Can this be His work? No, this is plainly one of the works of the soul.

I mention this extreme case in order to illustrate through an "extreme" how we may fly off on a tangent by just two or three degrees of incorrectness. When Mr. Barlow (a beloved fellow-Christian) was here meeting with us, one particular help I received from him was this observation of his: that in order to see if a thing is right or wrong, one only need magnify it to a hundred degrees, that is, have whatever it is drawn to the extreme. The guiding principle is that if it is wrong at the hundredth degree a person knows it is also wrong at the first or second degree. It is very difficult to judge by the first or second degree alone; in case there is any error such error is bound to be too minute to be discerned. But by lengthening or enlarging the situation or circumstance, everything will become most distinct.

A Chinese proverb runs like this: Missing by a hundredth or a thousandth of an inch will end up in a distance of a thousand miles. You may start with only a mistake of one hundredth or one thousandth of an inch and find yourself afterwards with a discrepancy of one thousand miles. Or conversely stated, by looking at the discrepancy of a thousand miles you can see the mistake at one hundredth or one thousandth of an inch.

Suppose there are two lines which are not exactly parallel but are off at a slight angle of one or two degrees hardly noticeable to the naked eye. If you lengthen these lines an inch longer the distance between them becomes obviously greater. Who knows how many hundreds of miles apart from each other these will be if these lines were to be extended to the ends of the earth? The distance at tens of thousands of miles away from their origin proves the existence of error formed at the starting point.

Now let us apply this rule to the so-called holy laugh. How do people get this laugh? What procedure do they follow, or what condition must they fulfill? It is nothing but simply the asking to laugh. There is but one thought, which is, to laugh. Are they seeking to be filled with the Holy Spirit? Their lips may indeed utter such words as "O God, fill me with Your Spirit." Nevertheless, that is merely a procedure; the aim of asking to be filled with the Spirit is something else than to be so filled. Though they may say so with their mouths, their heart desire is elsewhere. What is their aim? They want to laugh, to be joyful. They do not pray, "O God, I ask You to fill me with Your Spirit. I do not care for external sensation. If You fill me with Your Spirit, I am satisfied with or without feeling." Whoever wishes to be filled with God's Spirit ought to assume such an attitude.

Let me relate a true story. A student had repented and believed in the Lord. He had a fellow-student who professed to be filled with this holy laugh and seemed to be excessively joyful. This fellow-student urged him to seek to be filled with the Holy Spirit, saying how joyful he himself was from dawn to dusk without any sadness, and stating how helpful this experience would be to spiritual growth. Considering that his fellow-student was a believer and already a possessor of this experience, the recently-saved student thought he too should have it. Accordingly, he began to pray earnestly to God. He continued in prayer, asking God to give it to him; to such an extent that he lost his appetite and neglected his study.

Later on he went to see his teacher and asked that he pray for him. The student himself pleaded fervently with God, and vowed that he would not get up from prayer that evening if God did not give it to him. He kept on praying till suddenly he leaped up and shouted how joyful he was. He laughed and laughed. The more he laughed the funnier he felt. He laughed and danced and shouted. His teacher thought he must be out of his mind. Acting as though he were a physician, the teacher took hold of him and said, "Brother, be quiet, do not act disorderly." But the more he was admonished, the fiercer he reacted. His teacher dared not say anything more, being fearful lest he offend the Holy Spirit if this were truly of God. Finally the student went home and was better the next day. Now this was nothing but a great release of soul power, for he had fulfilled the condition for its release.

Example 6 — *Visions and Dreams*

Nowadays many people in the churches are seeking after visions and dreams. If any should ask me if I believe in them, I would reply that I do not oppose visions and dreams; I myself have had some experience of them. Sometimes they can be helpful. Yet I want to call your attention to their source. Where do they come from—are they of God or not of God?

How frequently in a meeting someone commences to tell of seeing a vision and this touches off an avalanche of visions until almost all in the congregation have testified to having seen visions and dreamed dreams. Hearing about visions, people begin to pray themselves, asking God to give them the same experience. They will fast and pray for several nights if a vision is not granted. Gradually their bodies will be weakened, their minds become blank, and their wills lose all power of resistance. They then receive what are called visions or dreams. No doubt they receive something, but how do they receive these visions and dreams? Are these from God? Such indulgence as letting the mind become blank and the will passive is definitely against the teaching of the Bible. They simply hypnotise themselves.

Some people are prone to dream, and they seem to be able to interpret their dreams, though often in a ludicrous way. I had a doctor friend who seemed to be able to dream easily. Each time I saw him I would be told of new dreams and their interpretations. He dreamed almost every night and frequently had three or four of them in one night. Why was this so? Was it because God desired so much to give him dreams? I know why. He was usually a day-dreamer, therefore he dreamed at night too. It was quite amazing to find so clever a doctor with such confused thoughts. His mind was continually drawing pictures from morning

till night. He had no way to control his thought. What
he dreamed at night was what he had thought about
during the day. Because of this I besought him most
directly that unless he resisted these many dreams he
would ultimately be deceived and his spiritual life
could not grow. Thank God, he grew better later on.
From this we know that many of the dreams are not
of God but are the effects of a scattered mind.

Examine the Source

Some seek for visions, some profess they have
seen light or flame, and some announce they have had
dreams. Following their testimonies, many others begin to claim they have had similar experiences. I do
not oppose these things, but I do probe as to their
origin. Do they come from the soul or from the spirit? Let us keep in mind that whatever is done in the
spirit, the soul can duplicate; but whatever is copied
by the soul serves no other purpose than to counterfeit the spirit. If we do not examine the source of
these phenomena, we will easily be deceived. The
most important point here is not to deny these things
but instead to examine them to see if they emerge
from the soul or from the spirit.

Differences in Effects

What is the difference in effects between the

operation of the spirit and that of the soul? This will
afford us a major clue in differentiating between what
is of the spirit and what is of the soul. "The first man
Adam became a living soul. The last Adam became a
life-giving spirit" (1 Cor. 15.45). Paul says here that
the first Adam became a living soul. The soul is alive.
It has its life, therefore it enables man to do all sorts
of things. This refers to the position which Adam
had. Then the apostle continues with: "the last Adam
became a life-giving spirit." This word is worthy of
close attention; it is most precious and significant.
The difference in effects between the operations of
the spirit and the soul is clearly given right here. The
soul is itself alive and has life in itself. The spirit,
however, is able to give life to others and cause them
to live. The soul is itself living, yet it cannot make
others live. But the spirit is not only living in itself, it
can also make others live. Only the spirit is capable of
quickening people into life. The soul, no matter how
strong it is, cannot impart life to others. "It is the
spirit," says the Lord, "that giveth life; the flesh
profiteth nothing" (John 6.63).

We must distinguish these two operations very
clearly, for this is of the utmost importance. None
can work satisfactorily if he is confused on this point.
Let me repeat: the soul is itself truly alive, but it
cannot make others to live. The spirit, on the other
hand, is not only itself living but in addition gives life
to others. This is why I state with such emphasis that
we must lay down our soul power. All that is of the
soul is of no avail. We are not quarreling over ter-

minologies, for this is too great a principle. Although the soul is alive, it has no way to make others live. Hence in helping people, we should aim at the depth of their beings instead of merely aiding their minds. We must not work according to psychic force, since it can neither save nor profit anyone. How very careful we need to be. How we must deny whatever comes out of the soul. For it not only cannot help people, it also hinders God's work. It offends God as well as deprives Him of His glory.

The Danger of Working in Soul Power

Let me use some common illustrations to show the difference between the workings of the spirit and of the soul. And again, I will not mention those miraculous cases because I have already touched upon them. We may say that it is quite customary in the church today to work by psychic means. How often psychological methods are used in ministry meetings to attract people! How psychic ways are engaged in in believers' meetings to stimulate the audience. By observing the methods used, one can judge what kind of work is being done. Let me say frankly that many sermons can only help people's souls, but not their spirits. Such messages are merely spoken out of the soul, hence they can only reach man's soul and afford him a little more mental knowledge. We ought not labor this way, because such work never penetrates into man's spirit.

How are many revival meetings conducted? (I am not against the reviving of believers, this I must make abundantly clear. I am only asking if the way of conducting such meetings today is of the spirit.) Is it not true that in many revival gatherings a kind of atmosphere is first created to make people feel warm and excited? A chorus is repeated again and again to warm up the audience. A few stirring stories are told to precipitate the giving of testimonies. These are methods and tactics, but not the power of the Holy Spirit. When an atmosphere is almost fully heated up, the preacher will then stand up and preach. As he is preaching he is already aware of the kind of result he will achieve that day. He has various strategies ready. By clever maneuvering he can anticipate that a certain class of people will shiver and another class of people will cry—that there will be confession and the making of resolutions.

Such type of revival needs to be renewed every one or two years because the effect of the medicine given previously will wear off and the old condition return. Sometimes the effect of an earlier revival will even fade away after only a few weeks or a few months. Great zeal and willingness are indeed exhibited at the start of a revival, but after a while everything is over and done with. This is due to no other reason than a lack of life.

If the stories of many believers were ever recorded, they would comprise a history of revivals: revivals after falls, and falls after revivals. The stimulant used at the first revival has to be increased in dosage for the second one. In order to be effective, the method employed in the second instance must be more emotional and more stirring. I would therefore suggest that this kind of method could best be described as an injection of "spiritual morphine." It needs to be injected time and again. It is evident that the soul can only live by itself, it has not the power to make others live. Working through soul power— even if people weep, make resolutions, and become zealous—is, practically speaking, worth nothing.

The Spirit Gives Life

What is regeneration? It is receiving the resurrection life of the Lord. Why does the Bible say we are regenerated through the resurrection of the Lord instead of the birth of the Lord? Because the new life received is more than the life of Bethlehem. That life which is born in Bethlehem was yet to die, but the resurrection life never dies. "I am . . . the Living one; and I was dead, and behold, I am alive for evermore" (Rev. 1.17,18). The resurrection life never dies but lives forever. The life that is born is in the flesh, it can therefore die. What we receive at regeneration is life which lives forever and never dies.

What is resurrection? Let us suppose that here lies a corpse. It is absolutely impossible to raise up the dead by human means. No matter how much energy is exerted and heat used, the dead will not come to life. The only way to make it live is to put God's life into it. This life which quickens the dead is resurrection life. And this is resurrection.

What environment is worse than death? What is colder than death? A corpse will deteriorate and decay more and more. But when resurrection life is infused, death is swallowed up by life. Consequently, a regenerated person is able to resist whatever belongs to death and is able to cast off all dead things.

The following is an illustration which has sometimes been used to explain resurrection. There was once a man who did not believe in resurrection. He was a very important person among a circle of atheists. After he died, the epitaph on his tombstone read: "Unbreakable tomb". The tomb had been built with marble. Most surprisingly, that huge marble sarcophagus was one day split open. It so happened that an acorn had fallen into the crevice of the stones during construction. It gradually grew into a big oak tree, and eventually burst the tomb wide open. A tree has life, hence it can burst open a place of death. Life alone can conquer death. This is regeneration, this is resurrection.

The spirit quickens; it alone can impart life. This is what we need to notice. But unfortunately there are too many substitutes for the spirit in our day.

Must Deal with the Soul

God only works with His own strength; consequently we must ask Him to bind our soul life. Each time we work for God, we need to first deal with ourselves, setting ourselves aside. We should lay down our talents and our strong points. We should ask God to bind these things. We should say to Him: "O God, I want You to work, I do not want to depend on my talent and my power. I ask You Yourself to do the work, for by myself I can do nothing."

Today many workers consider God's power to be insufficient so they add in their own. Work on such a basis is not only unprofitable but also harmful. Do remember that the work of the Holy Spirit never tolerates the meddling of man's hand. I often say that in God's work man should be like a paper figure which is lifeless and capable of doing nothing. He needs an influx of life to enable him to work. Let us deny ourselves to the degree that we become like paper figures, having no power at all in ourselves. All power must come from above; all methods used must also come from above. We know the Spirit alone quickens. God works by the Spirit. If we desire God to work, we must ask Him to bind our soul life; otherwise He is not free to work.

"Verily, verily, I say unto you, Except a grain of wheat fall into the earth and die, it abideth by itself alone; but if it die, it beareth much fruit. He that loveth his life loseth it; and he that hateth his life in this world shall keep it unto life eternal" (John 12.24,25). The word "life" here in the Greek points to the "soul". It means that whosoever desires to preserve his soul life shall lose his soul life; but whosoever loses his soul life shall keep his soul life to life eternal. This is a singular command of the Lord. He speaks in such terms so as to explain the meaning of the preceding words, "Except a grain of wheat fall into the earth and die, it abideth by itself alone; but if it die, it beareth much fruit." First die, then something happens. If a believer does not set aside his own soul life, the spirit will never be able to work and so profit other people. In order to perform deeper work for the Lord we must deal practically with the soul. The soul life needs to be lost. A grain of wheat is good and its golden color looks very nice. But if it is laid on a table, it remains one grain even until a hundred years later. It will never add one more grain. All our soul powers are like that grain of wheat which has not fallen into the earth. It can never produce fruit.

May we look at this problem with all seriousness. Does that resurrection life, which is holy and without blemish and which you now possess, bear much fruit? Some ask why they are unable to help or to save people? Some inquire why they lack power in work? Many confess they do not have power. But I will answer that they have no power to work because their own power is too great. Since they already possess great strength in themselves, where is the opportunity for God to work? By using their own wisdom, method, strength, or natural ability, believers block the manifestation of God's power.

Many miraculous phenomena are performed by soul force instead of by God. How can they expect good and lasting results if they substitute for the power of God their own natural abilities? Many revival meetings may appear very successful at the moment, but they drop to zero in effectiveness afterwards. No doubt some revivals do help people. But what I am referring to here are those works done through human methods. May I most solemnly declare that whoever aims at better and deeper work ought not speak of power. Our responsibility is to fall into the earth and die. If we die, then bearing fruit is most natural.

What does the Lord say about the one who loses his life, that is, the one who hates his life in this world? He will keep it unto life eternal. It is as though I have eloquence, yet I am unwilling to use it. My heart is not set on eloquence—I will not use it as my working instrument—I lose my eloquence— I refuse to depend on it. And what is the result? I gain life; that is, I am able to help others in life. It is the same with respect to my having managerial ability or any other ability but denying the use of it. I wait before God instead. Thus will I do people real good. Let us therefore learn not to use our own power so that we may bear much fruit.

Power ought to be obtained on resurrection ground. Resurrection is living beyond death. What we need is not greater power but deeper death. We must resist all natural powers. Whoever has not lost his soul life knows nothing of power. But the one who has passed through death is in possession of life. Whoever loses his own soul life just as a grain of wheat falls into the earth and dies shall grow in the life of God and shall bear much fruit.

I believe many people are so rich and strong that they give no ground for God to work. I frequently recall the words, "helpless and hopeless." I must tell God, "All that I have is Yours, I myself have nothing. Apart from You I am truly helpless and hopeless." We need to have such a dependent attitude towards God that it is as if we cannot inhale or exhale without Him. In this way we shall see that our power as well as our holiness all come from Him. Whatever we have is from Him. Oh how God delights in seeing us coming hopeless and helpless to Him.

A brother once asked me, "What is the condition for the working of the Holy Spirit?" To which I replied that the Holy Spirit never engages the help of soul power. The Holy Spirit must first bring us to a place where we can do nothing by ourselves. Let us learn to deny all which comes from our natural selves. Whether miraculous or common, we must deny whatever does not come from God. God will then display His power to accomplish that which He has intended to do.

The Lord's Example

"Jesus therefore answered and said unto them, Verily, verily, I say unto you, The Son can do nothing of himself, but what he seeth the Father doing: for what things soever he doeth, these the Son also doeth in like manner" (John 5.19). The Son can do nothing *of Himself.* In other words, of all the things which the Lord has done, not a single one of them is done by Himself. This is our Lord's continual attitude. He does nothing by His own power or according to His own idea. Whatever would come from Him is what He denies to do. Yet is there anything wrong with *His* soul? Is not *His* soul power quite usable? Since He has not the slightest trace of sin, it would not be sinful for Him to use His soul power. Nonetheless, He affirms that the Son can do nothing of Himself. If such a holy and perfect Lord as He refuses to use His own power, how about us?

The Lord is so perfect, yet His whole life is one which depends helplessly and hopelessly on God. He comes to the world to do the Father's will in all things. We who are but a speck of dust are really nothing. We must set aside psychic force and deny whatever comes from the soul before we can work with spiritual force and bear much fruit. May God bless us.